Impact of Artificial Intelligence on Public Accounting in Colombia

Transformation, Regulatory Frameworks and Implementation Strategies

Andrea Karabell Vega Florez

Impact of Artificial Intelligence on Public Accounting in Colombia

Transformation, Regulatory Frameworks and Implementation Strategies

ELIVA PRESS

ISBN: 978-99993-4-489-0

Cover Design: Eliva Press
Cover Image: www.ingimage.com
Email: info@elivapress.com
Website: www.elivapress.com

This Eliva Press imprint is published by the registered company Eliva Press Global Ltd. part of Eliva Press S.R.L. Publishing Group

The registered company address is: Pope Hennessy Street Level 2, Hennessy Tower Port Louis, Mauritius
Eliva Press S.R.L. Publishing Group legal address is: Bd. Cuza-Voda 1/4 of. 21, Chisinau, Moldova, Europe

Impact of Artificial Intelligence on Public Accounting in Colombia: Transformation, Regulatory Frameworks and Implementation Strategies

ABSTRACT

This research conducts a rigorous analysis of the impact of Artificial Intelligence (AI) on the efficiency and accuracy of accounting and financial reporting in Colombia. In line with the Industry 4.0 paradigm, a qualitative methodology of descriptive-deductive scope was used, based on a systematic literature review that included 54 authors indexed in Scopus and Google Scholar. The study assesses the transition from manual processes to automated ecosystems, examining how technological adoption redefines the praxis of the CPA. The findings underscore that, although AI optimises the quality of financial information, its implementation in the Colombian business fabric is slowed down by structural barriers such as resistance to change, asymmetry in technological investment, and training gaps. It is concluded that AI is not a mere peripheral tool, but a strategic imperative that requires a reconfiguration of professional skills towards high-value advice and predictive analytics.

Acknowledgements

This research work is dedicated with the deepest admiration and academic respect to **Dr. Maria Luisa Piraquive** for her support in difficult times and to **Magister Rosalba Flórez Flórez** for being my mother and friend, her tireless work in favour of educational excellence and her commitment to the formation of people endowed with ethical integrity and avant-garde vision constitute the foundation on which this analysis is built, her leadership is, and will always be, a source of inspiration for the positive transformation of Colombian society.

Dedication

I express my deepest gratitude to Professor Magister Mayeth Lizeth Duran Duran, whose expert advice and academic rigour were the compass that guided this research towards excellence. To my colleague Celia Zuley Peña Mendoza, for her invaluable collaboration, critical debate and constant support during the exhaustive research days.

Special recognition to the Technological Units of Santander (UTS) and to Magister Norelba Hernandez Mendoza, coordinator of the institution, for facilitating the academic ecosystem and the necessary resources to deepen the digital transformation of the financial sector.

My sincere thanks to Engineer Raul Flórez Flórez, CEO of ISL S.A., and Engineer Clara Inés Rojas Lizacano, CTO of the organization, for their avant-garde vision and for allowing access to real operating environments. To the company ISL S.A. and the Enterprise® Platform, for being fundamental technological references to contrast the theory with the praxis of modern accounting in Colombia.

Finally, I thank the Flórez and Vega families for their support and presence throughout every stage of my life.

TABLE OF CONTENTS

LIST OF FIGURES

LIST OF TABLES

EXECUTIVE SUMMARY

This study focuses on analyzing the impact of artificial intelligence (AI) on the accounting profession in Colombia through a literature review between 2021 and 2023. The objective of the monograph was to analyze the application of artificial intelligence in the preparation of accounting and financial reports in Colombia for its impact on the accounting profession. This analysis evaluated how AI affects the efficiency and accuracy of financial reporting compared to traditional methods, as well as the implications of its application in the accounting profession. Using a qualitative, descriptive, deductive methodology, information was collected from a bibliographic query in Scopus and Google Scholar. An analysis of existing findings was conducted to better understand the impact of AI on accounting in Colombia. In terms of results, this monograph made it possible to understand that the adoption of AI generates great results for companies, whether in the accounting area or in other dependencies; however, it is necessary to address barriers such as fear, change, lack of investment in new technologies, and the absence of training of workers to achieve the great results provided by the adoption of AI in organizations.

Finally, it was concluded that AI is essential in improving the efficiency and accuracy of financial reporting, as well as the need for accounting professionals and the technological infrastructure of companies to adapt to this technology. This study offers a comprehensive view of the influence of AI on the Colombian accounting profession and provides recommendations based on the literature review for future implementation.

KEY WORDS. Artificial Intelligence, Accounting, Financial Reporting, Colombia, Accounting Profession.

INTRODUCTION

The growing adoption of disruptive technologies, such as artificial intelligence (AI), is rapidly transforming various sectors of the global economy, and accounting is no exception. In this context, this degree work focuses on exploring the impact of artificial intelligence on the accounting processes of Colombian companies. The implementation of AI in accounting has led to significant changes in the way financial data is managed and analyzed, posing new challenges and opportunities for accounting professionals.

The integration of artificial intelligence across different sectors has radically transformed the way organizations approach their processes and make decisions. In this context, the accounting field is no exception. Automation, predictive analytics, and other AI capabilities are revolutionizing the way accounting is conducted, enabling greater efficiency, accuracy, and the ability to analyze. This degree project focuses on exploring the impact of artificial intelligence on accounting, as well as identifying the opportunities and challenges that this technology presents for accounting professionals and organizations in Colombia.

Through an analysis, it seeks to understand how these technologies are transforming job roles, business practices and the skills required in the accounting field in Colombia. This study not only seeks to identify the benefits and challenges associated with the adoption of AI in accounting but also to provide practical recommendations to optimize its implementation and make the most of its advantages in the Colombian business context.

1. DESCRIPTION OF THE RESEARCH WORK

1.1. PROBLEM STATEMENT

Technological advancement and the advent of artificial intelligence are rapidly transforming the way businesses conduct their operations and make decisions. In the case of the work of the Public Accountant in Colombia, it is presented as a potentially revolutionary tool that can significantly speed up and improve the process of analysis and presentation of financial information. However, there are also concerns about the impact this technology may have on the CPA job market.

The field of accounting has evolved alongside technological advances, and artificial intelligence has been one of the most influential innovations. In recent years, significant developments have been presented in the application of AI in accounting, which has generated an urgent need to know its impact. Institutions such as the National Institute of Public Accountants highlight how the adoption of these tools can automate accounting tasks, improving efficiency and accuracy in the delivery of reports and decision-making. (INCP, 2020)

This analysis not only focuses on the observed changes but also on the challenges and opportunities that these changes present to public accountants in Colombia. Authors such as the Fourth Industrial Revolution and the need for professionals to update themselves, leaving aside the routine activities of their daily work, to adopt a more leading role in financial and tax decision-making, facing new challenges. (Sánchez, 2020)

However, there are also challenges associated with AI in the accounting field. One of them is the fear that the automation of tasks could lead to job losses for public accountants or the ethical concern of how to properly use data and the implications of AI in terms of privacy and security, which is why the following question arises: How is artificial intelligence applied in the preparation and analysis of accounting and financial reports in Colombia?

1.2. JUSTIFICATION

This research is relevant not only because of its analysis of AI use in accounting, but also because it relies on a platform whose development lifecycle has been optimized through AI. This ensures that technological innovation transforms accounting processes from their very architecture, generating a positive impact on business productivity.The work of the public accountant is one of the oldest, it is characterized by being able to register, classify, interpret and analyze the transactions of companies, these actions to this day have been carried out by professionals who additionally generate reports and tax returns; Within this profession there are activities that are carried out repetitively so that digital tools have been created and of which they have helped to reduce this work a little and generate it more quickly and accurately.

AI as a digital tool has demonstrated its ability to automate repetitive tasks, improve accuracy in data management and increase efficiency in accuracy in reporting, this poses a window in which accountants can adopt and take advantage of the advantages for the benefit of customers and companies, As mentioned by the Many professionals and firms mention that these developments can help improve the quality of work and companies in the future. (INCP, 2020)

Colombia, like other countries, is experiencing an increase in business competitiveness. For this, AI helps professionals automate repetitive tasks and free up time to perform tasks that give added value to customers and invest in growth strategies, as mentioned, although there are also security challenges in the collection and management of financial information that require responsibility and transparency. (Heidrich, 2023)

The project on the application of AI in the field of public accounting is relevant for several reasons. First of all, studying the implementation of digital tools such as AI in accounting management not only helps to modernize traditional processes, but it also prepares students to face a constantly evolving labour market, where skills in technology are increasingly valued. This relevance translates into the student's daily life by providing knowledge about the practical skills with the greatest demand in the current labour field, which increases their employability and competitiveness in the productive sector. If the student is aware of the barriers that must be overcome to adopt AI in companies, in their daily working life, they will be able to identify when they are facing one of these obstacles and will be able to apply the tools acquired in their academic training and in the findings of this monograph.

In addition, the project contributes significantly to the field of knowledge by exploring how AI can improve efficiency and accuracy in business accounting, benefiting companies by optimizing their internal processes, facilitating decision-making, and contributing to the advancement of knowledge in the area of accounting and technology.

This project represents an opportunity to explore new technological applications in a field traditionally associated with conventional methods. He contributes directly to his line of research by examining how technological innovation can transform and improve accounting processes, thus generating a positive impact on business efficiency and productivity.

1.3. OBJECTIVES

1.3.1. GENERAL OBJECTIVE

To analyze the application of artificial intelligence in the preparation of accounting and financial reports in Colombia, and its impact on the accounting profession.

1.3.2. SPECIFIC OBJECTIVES

- To carry out a literature review on artificial intelligence used in the preparation and analysis of accounting and financial reports in Colombia.
- To evaluate the impact of artificial intelligence on the efficiency and accuracy of accounting and financial reporting and analysis in Colombia, and to compare it with traditional methods.
- To determine the implications of the application of artificial intelligence in the accounting profession in Colombia, and to understand how this technology is transforming the professional roles and skills required in this field.
- To formulate concrete recommendations for the effective implementation of artificial intelligence in Colombian accounting, thus optimizing the processes of preparation and analysis of financial reports.

2. FRAME OF REFERENCE

2.1 THEORETICAL FRAMEWORK

2.1.1. Artificial Intelligence.

Artificial Intelligence is defined as the ability of computers to perform activities that normally require human intelligence. AI is the ability of machines to use algorithms, learn from data, and make decisions based on that learning, similar to how a human would. AI-based machines can analyze large volumes of information without the need for rest and with a significantly lower proportion of errors than humans in similar activities (Rouhiainen, 2018)

In the realm of accounting and financial reporting, artificial intelligence has become a kind of powerful assistant that automates processes, improves accuracy, and gives us amazing insights from reams of data. You can think of process automation as having an incredibly efficient helper who takes care of all those repetitive and boring tasks in reporting, such as sorting transactions, balancing accounts, and generating financial statements. Not only does this save time and resources, but it also reduces those human errors that can creep in. (Mojica, Silvia, 2023)

The adoption of artificial intelligence in financial reporting leads to more efficiency and accuracy. Freeing accountants from those monotonous tasks so they can focus on what really matters, like strategically analyzing financial results and understanding what they mean. And thanks to AI's ability to process large amounts of data accurately, we reduce those annoying errors that can arise with manual data entry, thus improving the quality of our financial information. (Erazo, Muñoz, 2023)

The advent of artificial intelligence is changing the game for accountants in Colombia. It's no longer just about doing administrative tasks, but about becoming strategic advisors and analysts who use AI to deliver valuable insights to organizations. Of course, this also presents challenges. Accountants now have to acquire new skills, such as understanding how AI algorithms work and how to interpret the analytics they provide. That's why artificial intelligence is revolutionizing the way we prepare our financial reports. It makes us more efficient, more accurate, and helps us be more relevant in a constantly changing business world. (Wanden, Berghe, 2023)

2.1.2 Automation and Emerging Technologies in Accounting and Finance

New technologies are transforming the way financial data is handled, processed, and shared, opening doors to improving efficiency, accuracy, and clarity in accounting and financial tasks. Emerging technologies in accounting and finance are blockchain and artificial intelligence. These technologies are transforming accounting and financial processes, redefining the role of the accountant and promoting significant changes in the profession. (Vicente-Gomez, 2024)

Facilitating companies' access to emerging technologies, supporting them financially and establishing connections with customers and suppliers are key pillars to stimulate the emergence and growth of industries. These technological advances, particularly in the financial sphere, can promote transparency, improve interaction between government and citizens, and open new channels of communication. Legislation supporting the adoption of these new technologies is needed to strengthen the relationship between the government and citizens. (Valle-Cruz & Gil-García, 2022)

Artificial intelligence has the ability to stimulate the progress of complex companies in areas such as economics, finance, and accounting by processing vast amounts of information, making intelligent choices, and automating repetitive tasks. These technologies are radically changing the way accounting work is carried out. They simplify tasks such as recording financial transactions, generating financial statements, and managing payroll. In addition, they allow you to detect errors, identify financial inconsistencies, and monitor corporate loans. Automation can have negative repercussions in terms of job losses in various sectors; it also creates new job opportunities, although in variable ways and at different times. Technological advances are transforming the way accounting and financial activities are carried out, which implies that professionals in this field must adapt to these changes and be trained to face technological challenges in a globalized environment (Gónzalez-Murcia et al., 2022) (Meléndez, 2023)

2.1.3 Machine Learning

It is an important component to maintain business competitiveness and as a sales-enhancing tool in organizations. Machine learning refers to the ability of machines to learn from available data and improve their performance on particular tasks without needing to be explicitly programmed for each task. Machine learning simplifies the automation of activities linked to budgets, expense and income tracking, expense classification, financial flow analysis, and debt management, resulting in faster and more adaptable management of finances. This technology uses algorithms and statistical models to analyze financial data, make predictions, and make automated decisions (Brana et al., 2020). (Alfaro & Ospina, 2021)(Reyes-Delgado, 2023)

In the financial realm, machine learning technologies play a crucial role, and they fall mainly into three distinct categories. Supervised learning involves providing the algorithm with a set of labelled data, which makes it possible to predict certain outcomes. Unsupervised learning involves the algorithm working without the guidance of labels, seeking to identify similarities and group data autonomously. Likewise, reinforcement learning requires the algorithm to learn by interacting with its environment, receiving rewards for correct actions and punishments for incorrect actions, this approach is used in situations where the system needs to learn through trial and error, such as in digital currency stabilization, where the algorithm receives rewards for maintaining the stability of the currency in a volatile environment. These three categories of machine learning are critical to the development of more efficient and accurate financial solutions. (Villadangos del Río, 2021)

2.2 LEGAL FRAMEWORK

In Colombia, the adoption of Information and Communication Technologies (ICT) in public and private entities is key to the modernization and efficiency of the country. To regulate this process and ensure its proper implementation, specific regulations and guidelines have been established in the country. Table 1 mentions the rules governing the adoption of ICTs in the country's entities.

Table 1. Colombian Regulations Regarding ICT and AI Adoption

Regulation	Description
Law 2162 of 2021	**ARTICLE 7.** "Functions of the Ministry of Science, Technology and Innovation": paragraph 8 indicates the need to define the guidelines to be followed by government entities, public institutes and other bodies to carry out activities in the field of science, technology and innovation.
Law 1955 of 2019	**Article 147.** Public digital transformation. The state entities of the national order must incorporate the digital transformation component in their respective action plans following the standards defined for this purpose by the Ministry of Information and Communications Technologies
Law 1581 of 2012	**Personal Data Protection Law:** Indicates that it is essential to recognize and protect the right of all people to access, update and correct the information that has been collected about them in databases or files that can be processed by public and private entities.
Law 1221 of 2008	It establishes rules to promote and regulate Teleworking taking into account ICTs
Decree 338 of 2022	It establishes the general guidelines to strengthen the governance of digital security
Resolution 1117 of 2022	Establish digital transformation guidelines for the smart cities and territories strategies of territorial entities
Resolution 460 of 2022	Issues the National Data Infrastructure Plan and its roadmap

Resolution 500 of 2021	Establishes guidelines and standards for digital security
Resolution 2893 of 2020	It establishes guidelines for standardizing one-stop shops, specific portals for cross-cutting programs, electronic offices, procedures, OPAs (Citizen Service Offices) and requests for access to public information, as well as for integration into the Colombian State's Single Portal, along with other related measures."
Conpes 3975 of 2022. National Policy for Digital Transformation and Intelligence Artificial	It promotes the adoption of technologies associated with 4.0 industries by Colombian companies, such as IoT, Big Data, AI, robotics, virtual and augmented reality, additive manufacturing, nanotechnology and advanced materials
National Digital Transformation Strategy 2023-2026	It focuses on strengthening the enabling elements and promoting the use and appropriation of data and digital technologies in different sectors of society, addressing the challenges and risks associated with the acceleration of digitalization
Digital Colombia Agenda 2022-2026	It aims to digitally and productively transform the regions of Colombia, contributing to the change of the current digital culture and promoting connectivity, the development of digital skills and the democratization of ICT in all regions of the country

Source: Authors, 2024

2.2.1 Ethical framework for artificial intelligence in Colombia. (Minciencias, 2021)

Within the development of new technologies, there are various types of applications that for the national level need to establish certain parameters and guidelines in order to maintain order in the territory, for this Minciencias establishes an ethical framework focused on the development and good technological practices that avoid Effects on privacy, discrimination, misinformation, and maintain safety in users. Because when we talk about the advancement of artificial intelligence in Colombia, we are looking towards a future full of both economic and social promises. However, this path also leads us to face ethical challenges that demand our attention, to ensure that artificial intelligence is used responsibly and beneficially for all citizens.

2.2.2 Essential ethical principles

- **Transparency and Applicability**: It is crucial that artificial intelligence systems are transparent and their decisions are explainable. Citizens need to understand how these decisions are made and what data is used to do so. (Tierradentro, Rivera, 2023)
- **Fairness and Justice**: Artificial intelligence must be developed and applied in a way that promotes equity and social justice. This involves avoiding any unfair bias in algorithms and ensuring that all groups in society have equal access to the opportunities provided by AI. (Villadiego, Gonzalez, 2023)
- **Respect for Human Rights**: In the development and use of artificial intelligence, it is imperative to respect fundamental human rights, such as privacy, freedom of expression, and equality before the law.
- **Responsibility and Accountability**: Those involved in the development and use of artificial intelligence systems must be held accountable for their actions. They should establish appropriate mechanisms to monitor and evaluate the performance of these systems, as well as to correct possible errors or adverse effects.
- **Social benefit**: Artificial intelligence should be employed to promote public welfare and interest. Priority should be given to the development of AI applications that contribute to improving the quality of life of the population and the sustainable development of the country.

2.2.3 Particular ethical considerations for Colombia

- **Culture and Diversity**: AI must take into account Colombia's rich cultural and linguistic diversity. We must avoid simply importing models and algorithms developed in other contexts, and instead, promote the creation of solutions tailored to the specific needs of our society. (Tierradentro, Rivera, 2023)
- **Personal Data Protection**: The use of personal data in AI systems must comply with data protection laws and regulations in Colombia. It is essential to put in place adequate safeguards to ensure the privacy and security of citizens' personal information.
- **Inclusion and Accessibility**: All citizens, regardless of age, gender, ability, or geographic location, should have access to AI technologies. We must break down the barriers to their access and participation in the digital society.
- **Sustainable Development**: AI must contribute to the achievement of the United Nations Sustainable Development Goals in Colombia. We must encourage its application in areas such as health, education, the environment and infrastructure, to address the social and environmental challenges we face.

In short, for artificial intelligence in Colombia, it is essential to guarantee its development and use in an ethical, responsible way and for the benefit of society as a whole. This framework must constantly evolve and adapt to technological and social changes, with the participation of all relevant actors, including government, industry, academia and civil society.

2.3 CONCEPTUAL FRAMEWORK

2.3.1 Data Analysis in Accounting Reports

Data analysis in accounting reports refers to the process of examining and evaluating an organization's financial information in order to extract information and make strategic decisions. This analysis involves the use of various statistical techniques and analysis tools to identify significant trends, patterns, and relationships in financial data. By applying data analytics in accounting reports, companies can improve their understanding of their financial performance, identify areas of opportunity and risk, and make informed decisions to improve their profitability and competitiveness in the marketplace. In addition, analyzing data in accounting reports can also help detect irregularities or fraud, providing greater transparency and confidence in the financial information presented. (Flores, 2023)

2.3.2 Automation of accounting processes

Accounting process automation involves the use of technology to perform routine and repetitive accounting tasks more efficiently and accurately. This includes automating data capture and processing, account reconciliation, financial reporting, among other processes. By implementing automation in accounting processes, organizations can reduce time and resources spent on administrative tasks, minimize errors, and free up accounting professionals to focus on higher value-added activities, such as analyzing and interpreting financial information. (Cordoba, 2023)

2.3.3 Technological advances in accounting.

Technological advances in accounting refer to innovations and developments in the field of technology that are transforming the way accounting is conducted. This includes the use of specialized software, business management systems, artificial intelligence, blockchain, among other technologies. These advancements are improving the efficiency, accuracy, and accessibility of accounting processes, allowing organizations to manage and analyze large volumes of data more effectively, as well as adapt to an ever-changing and digitizing business environment. (García, 2023)

2.3.4 Digital Accounting in Colombia

Digital accounting in Colombia refers to the adoption and use of digital technologies in the accounting field by companies and professionals in the country. This includes the digitization of accounting processes, the use of cloud accounting software, the automation of tasks, the implementation of business management systems, among other aspects. Digital accounting offers numerous benefits, such as improving efficiency and accuracy in the management of financial information, reducing operating costs, and facilitating regulatory and tax compliance. In addition, it allows companies to adapt to an increasingly digitized and competitive business environment. (Acevedo, Ledesma, 2023)

2.3.5 Financial reporting efficiency with artificial intelligence

Financial reporting efficiency with artificial intelligence refers to the use of AI technologies to improve the process of generating, analyzing, and reporting financial information. AI makes it possible to automate manual and repetitive tasks, such as data collection and processing, identifying trends and patterns in financial reports. This leads to greater efficiency in financial reporting, reducing the time and resources required for its preparation, and improving the accuracy and quality of the information presented. (Ortega, Wasbrum, 2023)

2.3.6 Evolution of accounting with artificial intelligence

The evolution of accounting with artificial intelligence refers to the change and development in the field of accounting driven by the adoption and application of AI technologies. This includes the automation of accounting processes, advanced analysis of financial data, fraud detection, optimization of financial decisions, among other aspects. AI is transforming the way accounting is conducted, enabling organizations to be more efficient, accurate, and proactive in managing their financial information and decision-making. (Sánchez, 2020)

2.3.7 Technological innovation and accounting

Technological innovation in the Colombian accounting sector reaches a new level when AI is used to make the development of digital tools more efficient. By employing AI in the programming of the Enterprise Platform® software, a reduction in response times to regulatory changes is achieved, along with greater handling of large volumes of data, complying with Industry 4.0 standards. Technological innovation and accounting refer to the intersection between the development of new technologies and their application in the accounting field to improve the management and analysis of financial information. This includes the use of technologies such as artificial intelligence, blockchain, data analysis, among others, to automate accounting processes, improve the accuracy and quality of financial reports, and provide advanced insights for strategic decision-making. Technological innovation in accounting is driving significant changes in the accounting profession, allowing professionals to adapt to an increasingly digitized and competitive business environment. (Tierradentro, Rivera, 2023)

2.3.8 Artificial Intelligence in Accounting and Financial Reporting

Artificial intelligence in accounting and financial reporting refers to the use of algorithms and AI systems to automate and improve the process of preparing, analyzing, and reporting financial information. This includes automating routine accounting tasks, analyzing advanced financial data, detecting anomalies and trends, and generating customized, predictive reports. Artificial intelligence is transforming the way accounting reports are conducted, allowing organizations to be more efficient, accurate, and proactive in managing their financial information. (Villadiego, Gonzalez, 2023)

2.3.9 *Impact of artificial intelligence on accounting*

The impact of artificial intelligence on accounting refers to the consequences and changes resulting from the adoption and application of AI technologies in the accounting field. This includes improving efficiency and accuracy in financial reporting, reducing operational costs, detecting and preventing fraud, and transforming the roles and responsibilities of accounting professionals. Artificial intelligence is changing the way accounting is conducted, allowing organizations to adapt to an increasingly digitized and competitive business environment.(Tierradentro, Rivera, 2023)

2.4 LITERATURE REVIEW BACKGROUND

In the framework of this study, relevant antecedents at the international and national level are analyzed that provide a solid context to understand the research topic. An international background is examined together with two national antecedents, which offer varied perspectives on the subject and allow the identification of similarities, differences and trends in the field of study. These antecedents serve as a basis to contextualize the present research work and establish significant connections with the existing literature in the field.

As a reference, an international research was consulted, whose objective was to provide a meta-analysis of the literature review that involves a qualitative method to search and examine the literature on the impact of Artificial Intelligence applications on accounting and financial processes. The conclusions of the research indicated that most studies indicate a positive effect of the impact of AI systems on accounting and financial processes because they increase efficiency in all areas of accounting, especially those related to knowledge.

The aim of the paper was to provide an overview of the effects of the application of artificial intelligence on accounting and decision-making, to examine the changes and challenges associated with the adoption of these technologies, and to contribute to a broader understanding of how AI is transforming and redefining accounting processes and financial decision-making in today's world. The methodology used in the document was qualitative, descriptive, based on the collection of data and the presentation of results in a descriptive manner, without making inferences or generalizations beyond what was observed. Some techniques and tools used included direct observation, surveys, questionnaires, structured interviews, documentary analysis, and content analysis. The conclusions of the document indicate that the application of artificial intelligence in accounting and decision-making has generated significant impacts in these fields. AI has transformed accounting practices by automating routine tasks, improving data analysis, and generating personalized recommendations. Likewise, tangible benefits such as improved efficiency, reduced errors, and the ability to process large volumes of information quickly and accurately are mentioned.(Moreno & Balcázar, 2023)

On the other hand, the research whose objective was to determine the technological advances that have revolutionized the accounting system, as well as to show how these advances have contributed to the growth and improvement of accounting practices. The author used a qualitative methodology, basing the research on texts, essays, books and opinions of other authors. The conclusions highlight that the fourth industrial revolution has introduced significant advances in technology, which offer advantages that streamline and optimize processes, impacting various sectors such as transportation, commerce, health and economy. This technological revolution has transformed the perspective of activities that were previously carried out manually or with direct supervision. (Espitia-Melo, 2022)

3 RESEARCH DESIGN

This study was based on research with a qualitative descriptive approach. This type of research was chosen because it makes a detailed description of the adoption of AI in accounting processes in companies without manipulating variables or establishing causal relationships, which allows understanding the reality of the topic and compiling information in a single document. Likewise, the research is qualitative because it focuses on concepts and contexts that allow us to know the effects and reality of ICT adoption in the business environment.

According to the qualitative methodology, it refers to a research approach that focuses on understanding and analyzing social constructions through the analysis of discourses, representations, and meanings. It is highlighted that the qualitative methodology is responsible for studying the meaning and significance of social representations and discourses, through the analysis of the manifest content to reach the hidden or latent through interpretation (Pérez, 2002)

When addressing the issue of the application of artificial intelligence in Colombian accounting and its impact on the accounting profession, it is essential to understand the perceptions, interpretations, and meanings that the actors involved attribute to this phenomenon. The qualitative methodology allows for an in-depth exploration of these social and discursive constructions, providing a rich and detailed understanding of the topic at hand. In addition, as it is a relatively new and constantly evolving topic, such as the application of artificial intelligence in accounting, a qualitative approach allows us to capture the complexity and diversity of perspectives present in the academic literature and relevant documents.

A descriptive methodology focuses on the collection, organization, presentation and description of data or phenomena as they are presented in reality, without manipulation or intervention by the researcher. This approach seeks to characterize and explain in detail the characteristics or properties of a phenomenon, without necessarily looking for causal or explanatory relationships between variables.

In relation to the instrument used, the literature review is the main method used to collect and analyze relevant information. This method involves the search, selection, evaluation, and synthesis of previous research and academic works related to the subject of study. Through the literature review, it was possible to obtain a general and critical view of the current state of knowledge in the area of artificial intelligence applied to Colombian accounting, identifying both the main trends.

Content analysis was used to deepen the understanding of the application of artificial intelligence in Colombian accounting and its impact on the accounting profession. A literature review is a process where previous research and relevant academic papers on a specific topic are collected, evaluated, and synthesized. The main objective of a literature review is to provide an overview and critical view of the current state of knowledge in a particular area, identifying trends, gaps in research, and areas for future research. (Estrella, 2024)

On the other hand, the research establishes specific assumptions about the relationship between artificial intelligence and Colombian accounting, so it would be considered a deductive approach. This is because a deductive approach is based on a general theory or hypothesis that is sought to be proven or refuted through the collection and analysis of data. In this case, assumptions about how artificial intelligence might impact Colombian accounting act as a starting hypothesis, and the literature review would be used to gather evidence to support these assumptions.

4 DEVELOPMENT OF THE DEGREE PROJECT

Next, the activities for the analysis of the application of artificial intelligence in Colombian accounting and its impact on the accounting profession are observed. In order to meet the established objectives, four specific objectives have been outlined that guided the research and allowed the obtaining of significant results.

In Stage 1, a literature review was carried out on the application of artificial intelligence (AI) in the preparation and analysis of accounting and financial reports in Colombia. To this end, we identified relevant academic databases, journals and websites that contained information on this topic. Subsequently, systematic searches were carried out using key terms related to artificial intelligence, accounting and Colombia in the selected databases. The results of these searches were reviewed, prioritizing those articles, studies and documents published during the desired period of time.

Then, in Stage 2 of the methodology, a comparative analysis was carried out to evaluate the impact of artificial intelligence on the efficiency and accuracy of the preparation and analysis of accounting and financial reports in Colombia compared to traditional methods. To do this, a comprehensive review of traditional accounting tools was carried out and compared with modern tools that include artificial intelligence. Case studies and practical examples were examined that demonstrated the real impact of AI in the preparation and analysis of accounting and financial reports in Colombia, thus providing a complete vision of the advantages and challenges of the implementation of this technology in the accounting field.

Subsequently, in Stage 3 of the methodology, the implications of the application of artificial intelligence in the accounting profession in Colombia were determined to understand how this technology is transforming the professional roles and skills required in accounting. First, the skills that workers in accounting areas need to be competitive in an environment where artificial intelligence can be used in their work activities were identified. This involved conducting a detailed analysis of the skills needed to adapt and thrive in an automated work environment. In addition, the technologies that should be acquired to implement artificial intelligence in the accounting area of Colombian companies were identified.

Finally, in Stage 4, recommendations were made for the effective implementation of artificial intelligence in Colombian accounting to optimize the processes of preparation and analysis of financial reports. These recommendations are based on findings obtained in the earlier stages of the study. Specific barriers that could hinder the adoption of artificial intelligence in Colombian accounting were identified and addressed, such as a lack of staff training, resistance to change, and concerns about data privacy.

Table 2. Stages of information analysis

Stage	Activities
Stage 1. To carry out a literature review on artificial intelligence used for the preparation and analysis of accounting and financial reports in Colombia	• Identify relevant academic databases, specialized journals, and websites that contain information on the application of artificial intelligence in Colombian accounting. • Perform systematic searches using key terms related to artificial intelligence, accounting, and Colombia in the selected databases. • Select and critically review the relevant articles, studies and documents found. • Synthesize the information collected that clearly and in detail describes the current state of research in this field.
Stage 2. To evaluate the impact of artificial intelligence on the efficiency and accuracy of accounting and financial reporting and analysis in Colombia, and to compare it with traditional methods.	• To make a comparative analysis of traditional tools for the preparation and analysis of accounting and financial reports against modern tools that include artificial intelligence.
Stage 3. To determine the implications of the application of artificial intelligence in the accounting profession in Colombia, and to understand how this technology is transforming the professional roles and skills required in this field.	• Identify the skills required by accounting workers to be competitive in an environment that adopts Artificial Intelligence in their work activities in Colombia • Identify the technologies that should be acquired to implement Artificial Intelligence in the accounting area of Colombian companies.
Stage 4. Formulate concrete recommendations for the effective implementation of artificial intelligence in Colombian accounting, thus optimizing the processes of preparation and analysis of financial reports.	• Based on the above findings, formulate specific and concrete recommendations for the effective implementation of artificial intelligence in Colombian accounting, addressing the identified barriers and taking advantage of the available opportunities.

Source: Authors, 2024

5 RESULTS

Unlike traditional tools that rely on static programming, the Enterprise® platform emphasizes the implementation of AI to support the development team. This development methodology allows the software to be more accurate in detecting anomalies, overcoming the limitations of conventional accounting systems.

5.1 Application of artificial intelligence in the preparation and analysis of accounting and financial reports.

The IMA published a study on the impact of artificial intelligence on accounting and finance, based on the opinions of more than 40 experts. It reveals that AI is transforming the accounting profession globally by enhancing financial reporting, decision-making, and processes through automation. Accounting evolves into a strategic function. AI facilitates processes such as accounts payable and procurement and simplifies tax compliance, especially for international companies. In addition, it allows you to customize reports according to audiences. These changes offer new opportunities for accounting and finance professionals, who must develop technological and cognitive skills to leverage AI. (Ardila-Guerrero, 2024)

According to Pattnaik et al (2024), today there are several artificial intelligence technologies that are applied in the financial sector, specifically in the field of banking and financial services and insurance (BFSI). Some of the artificial intelligence technologies mentioned by the authors are described in the table below.

Table 3. Artificial intelligence technologies applied in the financial field.

Technology	Description
Data Analysis and *Business Intelligence*	Data analysis and *business intelligence* techniques are used to obtain information about the behaviour, preferences and needs of customers in financial institutions.
Predictive Modeling	Algorithms and statistical techniques are employed to analyze data and make predictions about future outcomes, helping to detect patterns and anomalies that may be indicative of fraudulent activity.
Internet of Things (IoT):	The use of IoT devices, such as health monitors, sensors, and GPS trackers, allows financial institutions to collect and analyze large amounts of data to develop predictive models and improve decision-making.
Natural Language Processing (NLP)	NLP techniques allow financial institutions to analyze and understand unstructured data, such as social media posts and customer reviews, to gain insights into customer preferences and sentiments.
Finance and Supply Chain Management:	Artificial intelligence and machine learning algorithms are applied to analyze data from financial statements and credit reports of suppliers, evaluating their creditworthiness, risk of default and facilitating access to financing based on their invoices.

Note. The information was obtained from (Pattnaik et al., 2024)

Artificial intelligence and machine learning have been used in recent studies to predict the stock market. These technologies make it possible not only to analyze different types of commonly used data and evaluation metrics but also to explore various neural network structures to improve the accuracy of predictions. Neural networks are especially well-suited for predictive analytics because of their hidden layers, in contrast to algorithms such as linear regression that use only input and output nodes to predict. The hidden layers in neural networks allow for more accurate predictions to be made when learning in a similar way to humans. Therefore, neural networks are a powerful tool for analyzing and predicting stock market behaviour (Najem et al., 2024).

The integration of AI into accounting and auditing processes has raised concerns about job replacement, especially in repetitive tasks. However, it has also created new opportunities for more qualified professionals, leading to a dynamic and knowledge-based accounting sector. AI can automate tasks such as math and data entry, allowing professionals to focus on critical thinking, strategic decision-making, and complex problem-solving. AI improves decision-making by analyzing large amounts of data, discovering real-time patterns, predicting future trends, improving financial forecasting, budgeting, and detecting fraudulent transactions. AI technologies encourage the adoption and use of AI in accounting activities, improving decision-making, automating procedures, and increasing overall efficiency.(Abdullah & Almaqtari, 2024)

Accounting practices can improve efficiency, accuracy, and strategic decision-making through modern technologies and by leveraging the capabilities of Industry 4.0. In Colombia, technologies and the industrial revolution are used to improve efficiency, transparency and accuracy in the management of financial information. Some ways in which these technologies are applied include automation of financial processes, which helps to streamline repetitive tasks and minimize errors in the processing of financial data, leading to greater efficiency in financial management. Likewise, the adoption of advanced accounting software allows companies to keep an accurate record of their financial transactions, generate detailed financial reports and facilitate compliance with accounting and tax regulations. Likewise, the digitization of financial documents and the implementation of document management platforms contribute to better organization and access to financial information, which facilitates decision-making based on accurate and up-to-date data. Data analysis tools and *Business Intelligence* they are also used to extract valuable information from large volumes of financial data, which allows companies to identify trends, patterns, and opportunities for improvement in their financial operations (Gaviria et al., 2022).

Artificial intelligence offers enhanced tools to project and analyze data with greater accuracy and less bias. This improves resource allocation and risk management, so it is considered essential to use statistical software and relevant technological applications to solve organizational management problems. In the case of Health Promotion Company, a company that operates in Colombia, it is argued that accurate and timely billing is crucial to avoid financial losses in health promotion companies, such as the Empresas Promotoras de Salud (EPS). Proper billing ensures that all services provided are properly recorded and billed, which helps ensure that the company receives appropriate payment for the medical services provided. Efficient invoicing helps identify and manage outstanding debts, allowing the company to maintain healthy cash flow and avoid the accumulation of bad debts. (Charris, Perez, Tovar, & Rey, 2024)

The adoption of Artificial Intelligence (AI) in Colombia has experienced significant growth in recent years, evidencing a fundamental change in the way companies and organizations approach their processes and operations. With the rapid technological evolution and increase in the availability of data, AI has emerged as a powerful tool for improving efficiency, accuracy, and decision-making in a variety of sectors. In Colombia, this trend is reflected in the progressive adoption of smart systems in areas such as health, education, commerce and, especially, in the business environment.

Figure 1. Artificial intelligence in Colombian companies

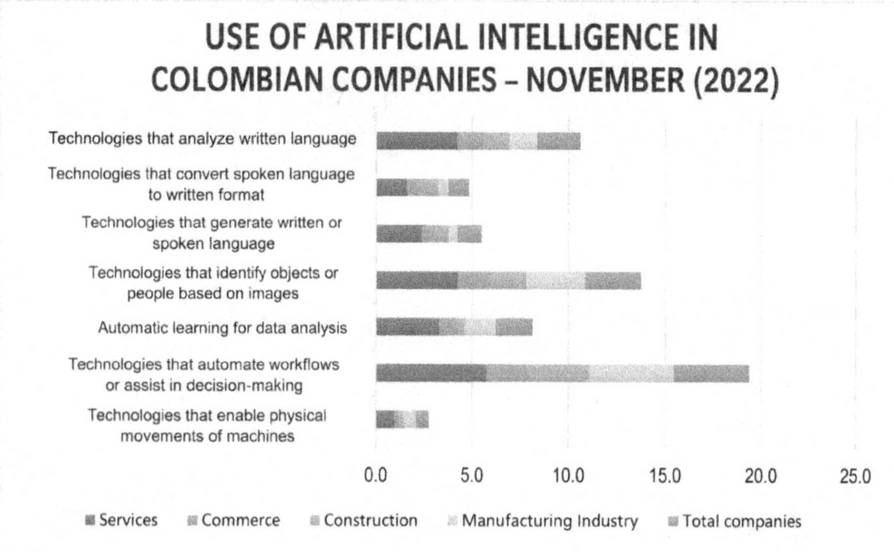

Note. The information was obtained from the Business Pulse Survey on organizations in Colombia with Artificial Intelligence implementations (DANE, 2022)

Below are figures on the implementation of artificial intelligence in its services.

Figure 2. Figures on AI implementation in Colombia

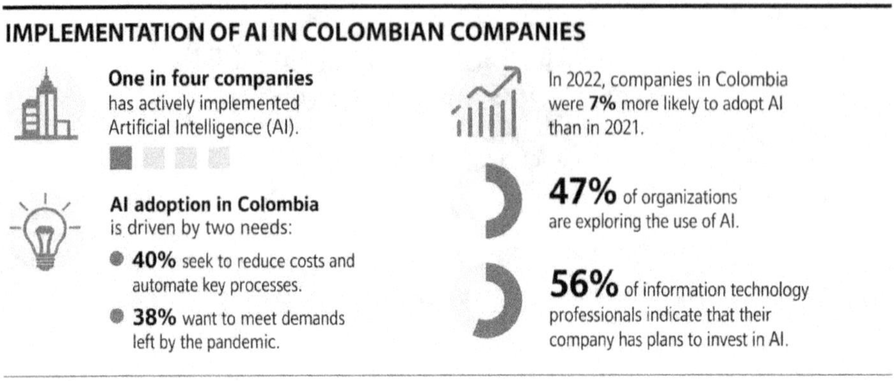

Source: The information was taken from the article published by La República. (Acosta- Argote, 2023)

Regarding financial institutions that have applied artificial intelligence, Financiera Comultrasan stands out with the introduction of "Fibot", a system based on artificial intelligence that streamlines the attention to queries and facilitates the generation of certificates and certificates for the company's associates. This tool handles more than 70,000 monthly interactions autonomously. (Acosta- Argote, 2023)

On the other hand, Finanzauto has implemented a comprehensive artificial intelligence model with the aim of deploying a predictive approach in its analysis. This model has the ability to examine both internal and external historical data of the company to anticipate possible operational scenarios, which facilitates quick and efficient decision-making. The organization has emphasized the importance of measuring and monitoring its processes as a fundamental part of this initiative.

In the business field, technologies that can help in accounting reporting include Artificial Intelligence (AI) and Business Intelligence (BI) technologies. These advanced technologies can improve transparency and efficiency in accounting reporting by offering detailed data analysis and predictive insights. Integrating AI and BI into accounting systems can enable family businesses to improve the quality of their financial reporting and meet more rigorous transparency standards. In Colombia, accounting and corporate governance practices can facilitate the rise of the company's financial conception. In addition, these technologies can be the solution to the crisis of confidence, especially through changes in accounting and auditing (Ramos et al, 2024).

Based on the information mentioned above and the ideas of the authors consulted, it can be deduced that AI has the ability to automate routine and repetitive accounting tasks, reducing time for accounting professionals, allowing them to focus on more strategic analysis and the interpretation of financial data. AI can use advanced algorithms to analyze large volumes of historical and current financial data, identifying patterns, trends, and relationships that might not be apparent to humans, making it easier to predict financial outcomes and helping businesses make informed, strategic decisions.

On the other hand, AI is capable of detecting anomalies or irregularities in financial data, such as fraud or accounting errors, through the analysis of unusual patterns and behaviours. AI can alert accounting professionals to potential problems, allowing quick action to mitigate risks and protect company assets.

Customization is an advantage that AI provides, thanks to the fact that it helps to generate financial reports adapted to the needs of each user. By using machine learning algorithms, AI is able to understand users' individual preferences and areas of interest, providing relevant and contextualized reports for each user.

The implementation of artificial intelligence in the preparation and analysis of accounting and financial reports can generate benefits for Colombia, the country's companies and its population in general. Among these benefits, the following stand out:

- **Greater business efficiency and competitiveness:** automating routine accounting tasks and allowing faster and more accurate analysis of financial data, Colombian companies can increase their operational efficiency and remain competitive in a globalized market, which favours companies to allocate more resources to innovation and business growth.
- **Improved decision-making**: The ability of artificial intelligence to analyze large volumes of financial data and predict future outcomes helps Colombian companies have a strategic advantage when making important business decisions, which can result in more informed and successful decisions to meet their objectives, which in turn can boost the country's economic growth and financial stability.
- **Reduced costs and increased profitability:** By automating accounting and financial processes, Colombian companies can reduce operational costs related to hiring staff and manual tasks, which leads to greater profitability and the ability to invest in initiatives that promote economic and social development in Colombia.
- **Early detection of fraud and errors:** AI can detect anomalies in financial data, which can help prevent fraud and accounting errors before they cause irreparable damage to businesses. This protects the assets of Colombian organizations and also promotes transparency and integrity in the business sector, contributing to a healthier and more trustworthy business climate in the country.
- **Generation of qualified employment**: the implementation of artificial intelligence can automate some accounting tasks and also create demand

for professionals with skills in data analysis, programming and technology management. This situation helps to boost job creation in sectors related to technology and information, providing job opportunities for the Colombian population and contributing to the development of a workforce with more skills that will allow them to grow in various sectors.

5.2 Impact of artificial intelligence on accounting and financial reporting

The advancement of technology, particularly in the field of artificial intelligence (AI), has revolutionized the way accounting tasks are carried out in businesses. Traditional accounting tools, once considered pillars in financial management, have undergone a significant transformation thanks to the integration of AI. The table below presents a comparison of how these tools have evolved and improved with the application of artificial intelligence, highlighting the benefits and new capabilities they offer for financial data management and analysis.

Table 4. Artificial intelligence in accounting tools.

Traditional tool	AI Tool
Spreadsheets (Excel)	AI-powered data analytics tools that enable more advanced and automated analysis of financial data, such as detecting trends and hidden patterns. • Tableau • IBM Watson Analytics • Microsoft Power BI • Oracle Analytics Cloud
Accounting Software (QuickBooks, SAP, Enterprise Platform®)	Intelligent ledger systems that use AI to streamline data entry, improve accuracy in calculations, and provide predictive analytics for decision-making. • SAP S/4HANA • Oracle ERP Cloud

Traditional tool	AI Tool
	• Microsoft Dynamics 365
Manual methods	Natural language processing (NLP) to analyse financial reports quickly and efficiently, extracting key information and generating automated text-based analysis. • IBM Watson Natural Language Understanding • Google Cloud Natural Language API • Amazon Comprehend
Manual Financial Analysis	Machine learning algorithms to perform advanced predictive analytics, identify financial trends, and detect anomalies in data more accurately and quickly. • IBM Watson Studio • TensorFlow, Scikit-learn • Microsoft Azure Machine Learning
Standard Reporting	Robotic Process Automation (RPA) for extracting data from multiple sources and generating custom reports in an automated way, reducing errors and work time. • UiPath • Automation Anywhere • Blue Prism • WorkFusion

Source: Authors, 2024

- **AI data analysis tools:** Artificial intelligence (AI) tools outperform Excel in several business-critical areas. For example, AI automates repetitive and complex tasks, reducing time spent on manual activities and minimizing errors. In addition, AI's ability to analyze large volumes of data quickly and efficiently allows businesses to identify hidden patterns and trends, which is not possible with Excel. This advanced analytical capability of AI also enables the generation of predictive insights, providing companies with deeper insight into their past and future performance. Finally, AI facilitates personalization in customer interaction by analyzing behavioural data and preferences, allowing companies to offer more relevant and engaging experiences (Islam et al., 2024).

  Among these tools is Tableau, which is a tool used in organizations for data visualization. Some companies own Tableau licenses, which allow them to create interactive dashboards, reports, and data visualizations in a user-friendly way. This tool is considered part of the Business Analytics (BA) technologies that are essential to facilitate the understanding of large volumes of complex data by decision-makers and other business users. Tableau easily integrates with various data sources, making it easy to connect and combine information from different systems and databases (Pedro et al., 2019).

Tableau is known to be a tool that has recently gained a good reputation within the administrative guild, thanks to the fact that it allows accountants to create interactive and personalized data visualizations, including graphs, tables, maps and dynamic dashboards, which facilitates the exploration and analysis of financial data. Likewise, Tableau allows accountants to identify trends, make forecasts and predict events based on financial data. Both Tableau and Power BI are usually very useful for accountants, however Tableau is usually more intuitive but Power BI has the great advantage of allowing integration with other Microsoft tools, such as Azure and SQL Server.

On the other hand, Power BI has advanced data analysis and visualization capabilities that allow users to create interactive reports and more sophisticated dashboards compared to Excel's capabilities. Power BI makes it easy to build custom business intelligence applications that can integrate data from a variety of sources and provide more dynamic and engaging visualizations than can be achieved with Excel. In addition, Power BI allows users to share and collaborate on reports and dashboards in real-time, encouraging collaboration and data-driven decision-making more efficiently than Excel (Bumblauskas et al., 2017).

Regarding Power BI, it has been observed that it can be a valuable tool for controllers, thanks to the fact that it allows advanced analysis of financial data almost intuitively and with great efficiency, due to the fact that it has interactive filters, data segmentation and trend analysis. Accountants can quickly identify patterns, trends, and relationships in data, making it easier to communicate findings and analysis to colleagues, bosses, managers, and clients to make strategic decisions. On the other hand, Power BI allows accountants to integrate financial data from multiple sources, including databases, Excel files, cloud services and business applications, which helps to have a comprehensive understanding of the financial situation of organizations, allowing data to be analyzed in a general way.

Another of the benefits of Power BI is that it facilitates collaborative work between all team members because it allows reports to be shared securely, guaranteeing transparency and collaboration within the organization, as all members have access to the same information that is updated.

- **Smart Accounting Systems:** SAP is an ERP (Enterprise Resource Planning) system widely used in companies to manage their business operations, while SAP S/4HANA is the latest and most advanced version of SAP. SAP S/4HANA is built on the SAP HANA in-memory platform, enabling it to process large volumes of data in real time and provide advanced analytical capabilities. Compared to SAP, S/4HANA offers greater speed, agility, and analytics capabilities, enabling businesses to make more informed and faster decisions. In addition, S/4HANA is designed to be more intuitive and user-friendly, improving the user experience and overall operational efficiency. By upgrading to SAP S/4HANA, there is an evolution in the role of the tax function in large multinationals. This update implies a shift in the tax function towards a more comprehensive and strategic approach to business, which improves tax management and adaptation to the changing needs of the business environment. (Pałys & Pałys, 2022)

- **Natural Language Processing (NLP) for Analyzing Financial Reports:** It is a field of artificial intelligence and computational linguistics that focuses on the interaction between computers and human language. The goal of NLP is to enable computers to effectively understand, interpret, and generate human language. This includes tasks such as text analysis, machine translation, text generation, speech recognition, and information extraction (Chung et al., 2023).

  The financial industry has been adopting technological advancements, such as Artificial Intelligence, Machine Learning, and Natural Language Processing (NLP), to improve people's financial well-being. In the last decade, the availability of unstructured datasets (such as texts, images, and videos) has piqued the interest of researchers to explore how these datasets can be used in the financial industry. For stock price prediction, researchers now use market sentiment data in addition to historical stock prices. Financial Natural Language Processing (FinNLP) deals with Natural Language Processing techniques applied to financial text data. (Ghosh & Naskar, 2023)

  There are various applications of NLP in finance, such as predicting exchange rates in the FOREX market, stock market prediction, customer relationship management, and cybersecurity. (Kumar & Ravi, 2016)

- **Machine Learning Algorithms for Financial Analysis:** Machine learning algorithms, especially supervised algorithms, play a critical role in developing intelligent information systems for financial analysis. These algorithms make it possible to predict financial trends, detect fraud, automate business operations, and provide financial advice to investors. In addition, it is highlighted that machine learning algorithms can analyze large data sets in a short time without the need for explicit programming, which improves the effectiveness of results in the financial sector (Lei et al., 2022). On the other hand, these algorithms outperform the traditional logistics model in predicting default risk, which can result in higher returns for investors (Liu et al., 2022). Accountants could integrate machine learning algorithms into their financial analysis due to the demonstrated ability of these models to predict with greater than 98% accuracy the risk of contagion in financial networks. This advanced tool allows them to identify and manage financial risks more effectively, improving the quality of forecasts and decisions (Samitas et al., 2020)

- **Robotic Process Automation (RPA):** Robotic Process Automation (RPA) in accounting and financial reporting from various perspectives. It is highlighted that as accounting firms move towards digitization, it is critical that they take data security seriously, especially when digitally storing client workpapers and information. Decentralization in information collection can present challenges for internal auditors, and RPA can help by enabling centralized collection of information, limiting who and how often sensitive data can be accessed. This can improve auditability, security, and address governance issues by limiting the use of unauthorized software that often leads to data breaches. RPA can help auditors save time in requesting, sorting, and extracting document details for further processing, which can be especially useful in audits of financial statements. Automation through RPA simplifies traditional manual processes, such as verifying disbursements with disbursement records and bank statements, allowing for faster completion of tasks such as collating information and identifying potential discrepancies (Perdana et al., 2023). The benefits of implementing Robotic Process Automation (RPA) in accounting firms include cost reduction, faster data processing, improved process control and performance visibility, higher data quality (accuracy, consistency, compliance), continuous operation (24 hours a day), and a positive impact on employees by freeing them from repetitive and mundane tasks. Common obstacles in implementing RPA in accounting firms include low adoption of RPA in accounting firms, limited knowledge of RPA capabilities and functionalities among accountants, accountants' fear of job loss due to RPA implementation, and the need for employee training and training in setting up software robots and automating manual tasks (Januszewski et al., 2021).

In Colombia, the adoption of artificial intelligence (AI)-based technologies is rapidly transforming accounting processes in various organizations. Next, financial institutions that have adopted AI in their accounting processes are observed.

Table 5. AI-based technologies applied in Colombia in accounting processes

Technology	**Company and description**
Data analysis with AI	• Bancolombia: It uses AI to analyze customer data to offer personalized products and services, such as fraud detection, risk management, and investment optimization. • BBVA Colombia: Implements AI to analyze market data and thus make better investment decisions. • Banco de Bogotá: Uses AI to analyze customer data to improve customer service and offer more relevant products and services. • SIIGO offers some basic data analysis tools, such as reporting and dashboard creation
Smart Accounting Systems	• Bancolombia: Use AI to automate accounting tasks, such as bank reconciliation and reporting.

Technology	Company and description
	• Banco de Bogotá: Implements AI to automate invoice accounting and tax management. • BBVA Colombia: Use AI to automate asset management and accounting fraud detection. • SIIGO Cloud ERP includes some intelligent accounting functions, such as automatic bank reconciliation and the generation of accounting entries
Natural Language Processing (NLP)	• Bancolombia: Use NLP to improve customer service through chatbots. • BBVA Colombia: Implements NLP to analyze customer interactions on social networks. • Banco Davivienda: Uses NLP to extract information from financial documents and thus improve the efficiency of accounting processes.
Machine Learning Algorithms	• Bancolombia: Uses machine learning algorithms to detect credit card fraud. • BBVA Colombia: Implements machine learning algorithms to optimize the pricing of financial products. • Banco de Bogotá: Uses machine learning algorithms for credit risk management.
Robotic Process Automation (RPA)	• Bancolombia: Uses RPA to automate repetitive tasks in its back-office processes, such as account opening and customer support. • BBVA Colombia: Implements RPA to automate document management and reporting. • Banco de Bogotá: Use RPA to automate bank reconciliation and payment management.

Source: Authors, 2024

Taking into account the information mentioned above, it can be deduced that the following aspects stand out in the impact of artificial intelligence on accounting and financial reporting:

- **Transformation of the accountant's role:** Accounting professionals go from being data collectors and processors to being strategic analysts and business advisors. Artificial intelligence focuses on repetitive tasks, allowing accountants to focus on interpreting data, identifying trends, and providing key information for companies to make strategic decisions.

- **Innovation and adaptation to technological changes:** Colombian companies that implement AI can differentiate themselves from their competitors, adapt more quickly to market changes, and lead the digital transformation in the accounting industry. This technological adaptation can be a catalyst for economic growth and boost business competitiveness nationally and internationally.
- **Ethics and responsibility in the use of data**: With the increase in automation and data analysis, ethical concerns regarding the privacy and security of financial data are being noted. It is essential that Colombian companies establish ethical policies for the handling of financial data that ensure the confidentiality, integrity and availability of information. It is also necessary that there is regulatory supervision to ensure that the use of artificial intelligence complies with ethical and legal standards and that it does not affect any person or organization.
- **Digital inclusion and professional training:** Accounting professionals need to be skilled in data analytics, artificial intelligence, and emerging technologies to stay relevant in an ever-evolving work environment; however, this training requires investments in education and training programs, as well as initiatives to promote digital literacy in the general population. As technology and best practices in the accounting field are changing, a culture of continuous learning needs to be fostered among accounting professionals, which involves participation in seminars, workshops, conferences, and refresher courses to keep up with technological advancements and market trends. In this area, it is crucial to ensure that all accountants have equitable access to education and technology opportunities, especially in rural areas or marginalized

communities, which requires investment in information and communication technology infrastructure, access to high-speed internet and affordable technological devices, and scholarship and grant programs to facilitate participation in educational programs.

5.3 Implications of artificial intelligence in accounting in Colombia.

When implementing artificial intelligence in the accounting of Colombian companies, several changes have been observed in the job roles and skills required. Some of these changes include:

- **Automating routine tasks:** With the introduction of artificial intelligence, many repetitive and manual tasks are automated, which can shift the focus of accountants' work towards more analytical and strategic activities. Artificial intelligence provides the opportunity for accountants to become strategic business partners by making it easier for organizations to become more data-oriented. This implies that accountants can play a more proactive role in business decision-making by leveraging the advanced data analytics provided by artificial intelligence (Kroon et al., 2021).
- **New responsibilities:** Accounting professionals can take on more strategic roles in interpreting data and making decisions based on more sophisticated analytics provided by artificial intelligence. Although artificial intelligence will automate routine tasks for accountants, it will also create new types of jobs that will require completely different skills. The remaining employees will be forced to focus on more strategic initiatives, such as process improvement, cost control, and capital optimization. In addition, the implementation of software in accounting with new functionalities, such as machine learning, optical character recognition, robotic process automation, and natural language processing, will allow faster manipulation of large volumes of data, reducing human errors and costs (Grosu et al., 2023).
- **Advanced analytical skills:** With the implementation of artificial intelligence, accountants need to develop advanced analytical skills to

interpret and make decisions based on large data sets generated by AI systems. It is critical for accountants to master the use of specialized accounting software, data analysis tools, and artificial intelligence systems to optimize financial information management and decision-making. With the vast amount of data available today, accountants must be able to analyze and interpret data effectively to identify trends, patterns, and opportunities for improvement in financial processes. Likewise, accountants must develop critical thinking skills to evaluate information objectively, identify potential problems, and propose innovative solutions in an ever-changing business environment (Norzelan et al., 2024).

- **Technical knowledge:** Greater technical knowledge is required to understand and operate artificial intelligence systems used in accounting. Greater technical knowledge is needed to understand and operate artificial intelligence systems used in accounting. This includes understanding algorithms, data analysis, and programming. (Zarei et al., 2023).
- **Adaptability to change:** The implementation of artificial intelligence in accounting systems implies a significant change in the way certain accounting tasks are carried out. This requires accounting professionals to be adaptable and willing to learn new skills and technologies in order to take full advantage of the capabilities of artificial intelligence in the accounting field (Yao & Jin, 2023)

Big Data, Cloud Computing and Deep Learning technologies have a positive and significant influence on accounting practices and the adoption of artificial intelligence in the accounting and auditing field. These technologies are positively associated with the acceptance and utilization of artificial intelligence in accounting and auditing, improving efficiency, accuracy, and decision-making in organizations. (Abdullah & Almaqtari, 2024)

The implications of artificial intelligence (AI) on the accounting profession in Colombia go beyond improving efficiency and accuracy in the handling of financial data. They also require a social and thought shift in a context where barriers such as fear of change and resistance to investing in technology can be prominent. AI drives everyone involved in the accounting guild to modernize and adapt to an ever-evolving business environment. To overcome these barriers of thought that hinder the adoption of changes that are convenient for the company, it is necessary to strengthen the following organizational aspects:

- **Change in organizational culture:** The implementation of AI in the accounting profession requires modifications in the organizational culture of Colombian companies, which implies promoting a mindset of openness towards innovation and change, as well as fostering a culture of continuous learning and adaptability. Organizations must be willing to challenge traditional practices and experiment with new technologies to stay competitive in an ever-evolving business environment. Fear of change and the "it's always been done this way" mentality are barriers that can hinder the adoption of artificial intelligence, these attitudes can arise due to comfort and familiarity with current processes and systems, as well as fear of the unknown and uncertainty about how AI will affect each worker's work and responsibilities.
- **Soft skills development:** In addition to the technical skills needed to handle AI, accounting professionals in Colombia will also need to develop soft skills such as creativity, problem-solving, and effective communication, which are essential to fully leverage the potential of AI and to collaborate effectively with colleagues and clients in complex problem-solving and strategic decision-making. By developing these skills, the fear that some professionals have regarding being left behind by technology and not being

competent because their work is already done by artificial intelligence is reduced. To fully exploit AI, human skills are required that a machine does not possess, so companies must encourage their employees to develop creativity in their jobs.

- **Change management and leadership**: AI in the accounting profession requires proactivity in change management and leadership from Colombian business leaders. The benefits of AI need to be clearly and effectively communicated, as well as any concerns and resistance that may arise among employees need to be addressed. Leaders must also be willing to take risks and promote a culture of experimentation and learning within their organizations. It is necessary for leaders to listen to their employees, take into account their ideas, concerns and alternatives to find together the appropriate use of AI that best suits the organization and its employees.

5.4 Implementation of artificial intelligence in Colombian accounting

The adoption of artificial intelligence (AI) technologies in Colombian companies implies overcoming barriers. Below are strategies recommended for companies to overcome these barriers and adopt AI in their accounting processes.

5.4.1 Resistance to change

This resistance on the part of employees and leaders of organizations is related to fears about the loss of control, changes in job responsibilities or the perception of threats to job stability. To address this barrier, the following strategies are proposed:

- **Communication and awareness:** It is essential to clearly and transparently communicate the benefits that AI can bring to the accounting department, such as the automation of repetitive tasks and the optimization of processes. Organizing awareness and training sessions for staff can help reduce resistance to change. If workers take ownership of the issue and know the benefits that artificial intelligence can provide to their daily work and how they can strengthen their personal skills, they may feel motivated to gradually adopt the use of AI.
- **Staff engagement:** Involving employees in the AI implementation process can help increase buy-in. Creating multidisciplinary teams that include employees from different hierarchical levels to work on implementation can foster a sense of ownership and commitment.
- **Recognition and rewards:** Design recognition and reward programs for workers who demonstrate a receptive attitude towards the implementation of AI and show a willingness to learn new skills that promote the efficiency of their work.
- **Accompaniment and support:** Provide continuous accompaniment during the implementation process, offering technical and emotional assistance to personnel facing difficulties. It is recommended that staff feel supported and understand how to change the way they do their work without falling into frustration or without affecting their self-esteem, by not being efficient by adopting artificial intelligence. It is necessary to remember that acquiring a new skill involves time and hours of effort, so the results are not immediate.

5.4.2 Lack of investment in technology

Investing in technology infrastructure, specialized software, and equipment can be costly and require a long-term commitment. Some entrepreneurs are unsure about risking large amounts of money on technologies that may become obsolete or are not urgently required; in contrast, they prefer to invest their resources in other areas and continue to use traditional tools. This thinking may be focused on immediacy, but in the long term, it is observed that companies that do not innovate are left behind. The following strategies are proposed below that can mitigate the risk of companies being overtaken by new startups or entities that implement technology in their processes.

- **Cost-benefit assessment:** A detailed analysis of the costs and benefits associated with implementing AI in the accounting department is recommended, which can help justify the investment to the company's management. This analysis should highlight the potential savings in time, resources, and human error that can be compelling.
- **Exploring financing options:** Researching external financing options, such as loans, grants, or government incentive programs for the implementation of innovative technologies, can help overcome domestic financial constraints.
- **Strategic partnerships:** Explore the possibility of establishing strategic partnerships with technology providers or companies specializing in AI that can offer affordable solutions tailored to the needs of the company.

5.4.3 Lack of training of employees on the use of AI technologies

The lack of adequate training and education of personnel on the use and management of artificial intelligence technologies can limit their adoption and effectiveness, which is why time and resources need to be dedicated to providing training and professional development programs that allow employees to acquire the necessary skills to work effectively with these technologies and maximize their potential in the business environment.

- **Customized training programs:** design specific and customized training programs for the staff of the accounting department, focusing on the skills needed to work with AI technologies, taking into account the particularities of each company, the skills of each worker and their respective job tasks.
- **On-the-job learning:** Promoting an on-the-job learning environment where employees have the opportunity to apply and practice the skills acquired in real-world situations. Likewise, it is necessary to encourage experimentation and teamwork to accelerate the process of adopting AI and for workers to feel supported and supported by their colleagues.
- **Mentorship:** Assigning mentors to employees who are learning to work with AI technologies can provide additional support and facilitate the learning process. Mentors can share their experience and provide one-on-one guidance. These tutors can be company workers, who know how the company works, the technology that the organization has and the goals for which all employees work.
- **Regular updates:** AI technology is constantly evolving, so it's important to provide regular updates on the latest trends, tools, and techniques in the field. Hosting refresher sessions and sharing educational resources can help keep staff informed and motivated to continue training.

6 CONCLUSIONS

- The adoption of artificial intelligence in the accounting profession in Colombia implies technological improvements and a cultural and mindset change. Overcoming fear of change and resistance to "it's always been done this way" is key to making the most of AI's potential and staying relevant in a changing business environment.

- It is concluded that the use of AI to optimize the development of accounting software is a differentiating factor driving the country's technological modernization. Companies like ISL S.A. demonstrate that efficiency in software creation is what allows the certified public accountant to finally fulfill their role.

- Promoting a culture of continuous learning, strong leadership, and collaboration between accounting professionals and technologists is necessary to facilitate the successful adoption of AI in the accounting profession in Colombia, which requires a commitment to education, awareness, and the development of technical and soft skills to adapt to changes and take advantage of the opportunities offered by AI to companies and their employees.

- The integration of artificial intelligence into accounting processes leads to a significant improvement in operational efficiency and the accuracy of financial analyses. The automation of repetitive tasks and the ability to analyze advanced data allow for a more agile and accurate execution of accounting operations.

- AI plays a critical role in reducing human errors in accounting, resulting in a significant decrease in costs related to correcting such errors. This cost reduction translates into increased profitability and greater efficiency in the financial management of organizations.

- The adoption of artificial intelligence in accounting motivates professionals in the sector to expand and update their skills, which contributes to their professional and personal development. The need to understand and work with AI tools drives continuous training and the improvement of technical and analytical skills.

- Companies that incorporate AI into their accounting processes are undergoing significant technological modernization. This upgrade allows them to keep up with the latest trends and advancements in technology, strengthening their competitive position in the market and providing them with a strategic advantage.

- AI in accounting not only improves efficiency and accuracy, but also drives innovation and business competitiveness. By enabling deeper and more detailed analysis of financial data, AI provides valuable insights for strategic decision-making, allowing organizations to quickly adapt to market changes and anticipate future needs.

7 RECOMMENDATIONS

- It is suggested to continue exploring updated and relevant research sources to keep up with the advances in the use of artificial intelligence in the world and in Colombian accounting. This will deepen knowledge on the subject and contribute to the development of the accounting profession in the country.
- It is essential to investigate technological developments and trends in the field of artificial intelligence and the impact of this technology on accounting processes. This will allow identifying opportunities for improvement and optimisation in the use of AI in the Colombian context.
- It is recommended to promote spaces for constant dialogue between accounting professionals, academics and technology experts to analyse and discuss the implications of AI in the accounting guild in Colombia to help generate a greater understanding of the changes in roles and skills required in the new dynamics of the labour market.
- Develop detailed and customised action plans for the implementation of artificial intelligence in Colombian organisations, taking into account their specific needs and technological capabilities, which requires establishing training strategies, change management policies, and data security protocols that ensure a successful and sustainable adoption of AI in the accounting field.

BIBLIOGRAPHIC REFERENCES

Abdullah, A. A., & Almaqtari, F. A. (2024). The impact of artificial intelligence and Industry 4.0 on transforming accounting and auditing practices. *Journal of Open Innovation: Technology, Market, and Complexity, 10(1)*, 100218.

Abdullah, A. A., & Almaqtari, F. A. (2024). The impact of artificial intelligence and Industry 4.0 on transforming accounting and auditing practices. . *Journal of Open Innovation: Technology, Market, and Complexity, 10(1).*

Acevedo, Ledesma. (2023). *Optimization of information and time in the generation of financial reports using business intelligence and data analysis tools in WTW Colombia.* Retrieved from https://repositorio.unicordoba.edu.co/entities/publication/6211498f-dd56-4da3-8afe-df698ea8a8e8

Acosta- Argote, C. (2023, September 26). *Colombian companies that have integrated artificial intelligence into their services.* Retrieved from La República: https://www.larepublica.co/especiales/revolucion-5-0/las-empresas-colombianas-que-han-integrado-la-inteligencia-artificial-a-sus-servicios-3713204

Alfaro, A. D., & Ospina, J. V. (2021). Systematic literature review: Machine learning techniques. *Active Notebook, 13(1),* 113-121.

Ardila-Guerrero, H. (March 5, 2024). *INCP.* Obtained from AI is transforming the finance and accounting function: https://incp.org.co/publicaciones/infoincp-publicaciones/2024/03/la-ia-esta-transformando-la-funcion-financiera-y-contable/

Braña, J. P., Litterio, A., & Fernández, A. (2020). Artificial intelligence and quantum computing in finance. *In XXII Workshop of Researchers in Computer Science (WICC 2020, El Calafate, Santa Cruz).*

Bumblauskas, D., Gemmill, D., Igou, A., & Anzengruber, J. (2017). Smart Maintenance Decision Support Systems (SMDSS) based on corporate big data analytics. *Expert systems with applications, 90*, 303-317.

Charris, N. N., Perez, E. B., Tovar, O. O., & Rey, D. D. (2024). Analysis of the Impact of Billing, Authorizations and Unknown Debts on the Technical Reserve of Health Promotion Companies: Case of HPC in Colombia. *Procedia Computer Science, 231,*, 607-614.

Chung, S., Moon, S., Kim, J., Kim, J., Lim, S., & Chi, S. (2023). Comparing natural language processing (NLP) applications in construction and computer science using preferred reporting items for systematic reviews (PRISMA). *Automation in Construction, 154*.

Cordoba. (2023). Technology Optimization: Automation and Data Analysis. *7*(17), 90. Retrieved from https://dspace.tdea.edu.co/handle/tdea/4164

DANE. (December 15, 2022). Retrieved from https://www.dane.gov.co/index.php/estadisticas-por-tema/comercio-interno/encuesta-pulso-empresarial

Erazo, Muñoz. (2023). Auditing of the future, foresight and artificial intelligence to anticipate risks in organizations. *6*(1), 105-119. Retrieved from http://scielo.senescyt.gob.ec/scielo.php?script=sci_arttext&pid=S2631-26542023000100105

Espitia-Melo, N. C. (2022). *Challenges in the accounting profession in the face of artificial intelligence.* Repository Cooperative University of Colombia.

Estrella, S. (2024). The tabular format: a literature review. *Actualidad investigativas en educación, 14(2)*, 449-478.

Flowers. (2023). Competencies in accounting processes, internal control, and general knowledge in accountants of religious entities in inter-American countries. *7*(15), 67. Retrieved from https://revistas.upeu.edu.pe/index.php/ri_va/article/view/2050

García. (2023). EFFECTS OF THE APPLICATION OF ARTIFICIAL INTELLIGENCE IN ACCOUNTING AND DECISION-MAKING. *7*(15), 70. Retrieved from https://revistap.ejeutap.edu.co/index.php/Gestion/article/view/71

Gaviria, D. A., Polo, O. C., Martínez, E. M., & García-Arango, D. A. (2022). Influence of the Fourth Industrial Revolution on the Ethics of the Colombian Accounting Professional. *Procedia Computer Science, 215*, 626-641.

Ghosh, S., & Naskar, S. K. (2023). Recent trends in financial natural language processing research. *Science Talks, 8.*

González-Murcia, A. Y., Romero-Melo, D. K., Corredor-Cifuentes, G. P.-F., & Suárez-Ibagué, J. S. (2022). *Impact of emerging technologies on the position of the accounting assistant (Bachelor's thesis, Public-Virtual Accounting).* Bogotá: EAN University Repository.

Grosu, V., Cosmulese, C. G., Socoliuc, M., Ciubotariu, M. S., & Mihaila, S. (2023). Testing accountants' perceptions of the digitization of the profession and profiling the future professional. *Technological Forecasting and Social Change, 193.*

Heidrich. (2023). *Artificial intelligence: the key to business competitiveness in the digital age.* . Retrieved from https://www.linkedin.com/pulse/la-inteligencia-artificial-clave-para-competitividad-empresarial/?originalSubdomain=es

INCP. (2020). AI is transforming the finance and accounting function. *4*(12), 50-62. Retrieved from https://incp.org.co/publicaciones/infoincp-publicaciones/2024/03/la-ia-esta-transformando-la-funcion-financiera-y-contable/

Islam, M. T., Hasan, M. M., Redwanuzzaman, M., & Hossain, M. K. (2024). Practices of artificial intelligence to improve the business in Bangladesh. *Social Sciences & Humanities Open, 9.*

Januszewski, A., Kujawski, J., & Buchalska-Sugajska, N. (2021). Benefits of and obstacles to RPA implementation in accounting firms. *Procedia Computer Science, 192*, 4672-4680.

Kroon, N., do Céu Alves, M., & Martins, I. (2021). The impacts of emerging technologies on accountants' role and skills: Connecting to open innovation—a systematic literature review. *Journal of Open Innovation: Technology, Market, and Complexity, 7(3)*, 163.

Kumar, B. S., & Ravi, V. (2016). A survey of the applications of text mining in financial domain. *Knowledge-Based Systems, 114*, 128-147.

Lei, X., Mohamad, U. H., Sarlan, A., Shutaywi, M., Daradkeh, Y. I., & Mohammed, H. O. (2022). Development of an intelligent information system for financial analysis depend on supervised machine learning algorithms. *Information Processing & Management, 59(5).*

Liu, Y., Yang, M., Wang, Y., Li, Y., Xiong, T., & Li, A. (2022). Applying machine learning algorithms to predict default probability in the online credit market: Evidence from China. *International Review of Financial Analysis, 79.*

Meléndez, J. R. (2023). Economics, finance and accounting. *Venezuelan Journal of Management: RVG, 28(103)*, 930-931.

Mojica, Silvia. (2023). Artificial Intelligence in External Auditing: Analysis of new technologies in the design of documentation for the management of the financial auditor of the new era. *4*(12), 100. Retrieved from https://repository.unab.edu.co/handle/20.500.12749/20151

Moreno, E. G., & Balcázar, M. D. (2023). Effects of the application of artificial intelligence in accounting and decision-making. *Management, 1(1).*

Najem, R., Amr, M. F., Bahnasse, A., & Talea, M. (2024). Advancements in Artificial Intelligence and Machine Learning for Stock Market Prediction: A Comprehensive Analysis of Techniques and Case Studies. *Procedia Computer Science, 231*, 198-204.

Norzelan, N. A., Mohamed, I. S., & Mohamad, M. (2024). Technology acceptance of artificial intelligence (AI) among heads of finance and accounting units in the shared service industry. *Technological Forecasting and Social Change, 198.*

Ortega, Wasbrum. (2023). *Managerial accounting as a tool for financial decision-making in the agro-export industry. Case: Quevedo* . Retrieved from https://www.ciencialatina.org/index.php/cienciala/article/view/6397

Pałys, A., & Pałys, M. (2022). The challenges for tax compliance in multinationals within the SAP environment. *Procedia Computer Science, 207*, 2384-2394.

Pattnaik, D., Ray, S., & Raman, R. (2024). Applications of artificial intelligence and machine learning in the financial services industry: A bibliometric review. *Heliyon.*

Pedro, J., Brown, I., & Hart, M. (2019). Capabilities and readiness for big data analytics. *Procedia Computer Science, 164*, 3-10.

Perdana, A., Lee, W. E., & Kim, C. M. (2023). Prototyping and implementing Robotic Process Automation in accounting firms: Benefits, challenges and opportunities to audit automation. *International Journal of Accounting Information Systems, 51.*

Pérez, A. C. (2002). On qualitative methodology. *Spanish Journal of Public Health, 76*, 373-380.

Ramos, L. N., Gutierrez, I., Vásquez, A. V., Calderón, L., Correa, K. R., & Beleño, C. G. (2024). Family business: transparency in financial information from corporate governance practices. *Procedia Computer Science, 231*, 484-489. Obtenido de Procedia Computer Science, 231.

Reyes-Delgado, J. C. (2023). *Proposal of a platform for the management of personal finances with Deep Learning.* Bogotá: Unipiloto Repository.

Rouhiainen, L. (2018). Artificial intelligence. *Madrid: Anima Editorial*, 20-21.

Samitas, A., Kampouris, E., & Kenourgios, D. (2020). Machine learning as an early warning system to predict financial crisis. *International Review of Financial Analysis, 71*.

Sánchez. (2020). ENVIRONMENTAL ACCOUNTING: A CHALLENGE FOR COMPREHENSIVE ACCOUNTING PROFESSIONAL TRAINING. *5*(12), 100. Retrieved from file:///Users/dayanamartinez/Downloads/ojstdea,+Articulo+1.+Contabilidad+ambiental.+VSLM+1+(2).pdf

Tierradentro, Rivera. (2023). Advances and perspectives of artificial intelligence applied to justice. *5*(12), 62. Retrieved from https://repository.unilibre.edu.co/handle/10901/28299

Valle-Cruz, D., & Gil-García, J. R. (2022). Emerging Ecnologies in Local Governments: A Systematic Literature Review with the PRISMA Methodology. *Mexican Journal of Political Analysis and Public Administration, 11(21),* 9-28.

Vicente-Gómez, D. (2024). *Emerging technologies in accounting: blockchain and artificial intelligence.* Madrid: Rey Juan Carlos Universidas Repository.

Villadangos del Río, Á. (2021). *Application of Machine Learning techniques in finance.* Comillas Repository.

Villadiego, González. (2023). Ethical considerations for the training of artificial intelligence engineers in Colombia. *5*(14), 90. Retrieved from https://repositorio.escuelaing.edu.co/handle/001/2810

Wanden, Berghe. (2023). Blockchain and artificial intelligence in the accounting information system: the disruption of the triple entry. *5*(12), 62. Retrieved from https://rua.ua.es/dspace/handle/10045/135180

Yao, L., & Jin, M. (2023). Research on Accounting Data Encryption Processing System based on Artificial Intelligence. *Procedia Computer Science, 228*, 373-382.

Zarei, E., Khan, F., & Abbassi, R. (2023). How to account artificial intelligence in human factor analysis of complex systems? *Process safety and environmental protection, 171*, 736-750.

Publisher: Eliva Press Global Ltd

Email: info@elivapress.com

www.ingramcontent.com/pod-product-compliance
Lightning Source LLC
LaVergne TN
LVHW022314200926
848481LV00004B/1333

9789999344890